KISA GOTAMI
a mother's sorrow

KISA GOTAMI
a mother's sorrow

Raj Arumugam

CONTENTS

Prologue

Prologue

Buddham Saranam Gacchami
Dhammam Saranam Gacchami
Sangham Saranam Gacchami

Listen to the story of Kisa Gotami.

Listen to the story of Kisa Gotami of Savatthi of the
kingdom of Kosala, of ancient India in the time of the
Buddha, the Enlightened One.

Listen to the story of Kisa Gotami, the mother who
suffered the death of her only child. Listen to her pain
and agony and how in that pain and agony, in her
suffering, was born her wisdom.

Listen to the story of Kisa Gotami's suffering and how
pain led to the abiding vision in her: *all things that arise
must cease.* All things end; that is the natural order of
things and it profits not to dwell on it. More useful it to
find the means to transcend samsara, to cross this ocean
of life, birth, transience and death.

Buddham Saranam Gacchami
Dhammam Saranam Gacchami
Sangham Saranam Gacchami

Scene 1
Gotami's child

NARRATOR

This is Savatthi, the capital city of the kingdom of Kosala, of ancient India in the time of the Buddha, the Enlightened One.

The city sleeps. Night passes and now the sun rises ever slowly.

One hears the sounds of the break of day.

One hears the bullock carts and the dogs and the cows and the early roosters.

The sun is not fully risen but already the hawkers and the stall-owners and the merchants at the city market are busy preparing for the day.

They make haste. The market is now open.

The sun has risen.

The hawkers and the stall-owners and the merchants are ready for another day.

Stall-owner

You are late this morning, Sujata. It is rare; it is not in character. Surely something unusual must have happened, Sujata, even so early in the morning.

Sujata

Something has happened, indeed. Something sad and tragic and that is the cause of my being late.

Stall-owner

Never have you been late, Sujata. Three years have you worked for me in this store and you have always been here right on time. What has happened, Sujata?

Sujata

It is Kisa Gotami.

Stall-owner

Kisa Gotami, your friend. Kisa Gotami the Thin One. Kisa Gotami the Frail One.

Sujata

Kisa Gotami, my friend. Kisa Gotami, my neighbor.
And indeed, Kisa Gotami the Thin One. Kisa Gotami the
Frail One.

Early this morning, even before the first rays of the sun,
there was a scream. And sobbing.

Kisa Gotami, I learned later, woke up to find her only
child dead beside her.
Kisa Gotami's only child, her son of six months, and
dead of cholera.

Kisa Gotami screams and cries.
And her husband says: *The child is dead.*
Kisa Gotami says: *No.*

And her mother-in-law says: *You are an orphan as you
started – your son is dead. You have no one again - your
son is dead. You came as an orphan, and you leave as
an orphan. Your son is dead.*

Yet Kisa Gotami says: *No. He is sick. He is not dead.*
And she screams and she beats herself and she scratches
her face, and she picks up her dead son, holds him
propped up against her on her hip as mothers of Savatthi
may carry their children, and she runs out into the
streets.
Give my son some medicine, she screams. *Cure him.*

People come out to see what the noise is all about.

Give my son some medicine, Kisa Gotami screams still.

He is dead, says one neighbor.

No, she says. *Cure him. Surely there must be some herbs to revive him.*

She sees me in the street. She runs to me.
Give my son some medicine, Sujata, she says to me.
I try to calm her. *Listen to me, Kisa,* I say. *Listen, my dear friend. Calm down.*

Kisa Gotami beats her forehead. She screams. She shouts: *My family will not help me. My neighbors will not help me. My friends will not help me. I will go to strangers who may. I begun my life as an orphan and here am I become an orphan again. To strangers must orphans go.*

And she runs away. And she runs carrying her child on her hip. She runs out of the neighborhood and she runs in her madness.

And then I came here.

Stall-owner

And here she comes, Sujata. Look, here comes your friend Kisa Gotami with her dead child propped up against her on her hip as mothers of Savatthi may carry their children. O, she carries her child as if he were still alive.

Kisa Gotami

O people of Savatthi. I am Kisa Gotami.

O strangers of Savatthi. O good people of Savatthi – listen to my grief.

I am Kisa Gotami.

Here I bear my child on my hip.
See my child, weak and helpless.
Help us, O good people of Savatthi.

Give my son some medicine.

Help me.

Help my son, O good people of Savatthi.

My husband will not help us. My mother-in-law will not help us. I have no parents or brothers or sisters to help me.

My neighbors will not help us. My friends will not help us.

They mock and they make fun of me. They say –
Cremate your child.
O, they are heartless – *Cremate your child*, they say.

He is not dead.

My son is not dead.

He needs medicine; he needs help.

Help us, good people of Savatthi.

Do not mock us.
Do not stand away from us.
O, sir, help me.
O, kind mother, you with that child by your side, surely
you know the grief of a mother. Help me. Help my child.

Will none of you help?

What is it you say, good people of Savatthi?
What is it you say?

You say my son is dead.

You say I am blind in my grief and do not know he is
dead.

Let it be so, good people of Savatthi. Let it be so, that he
is dead.
My son is dead. You see, I say the same thing you say.
My son is dead, but help us, good people.

See, I admit he is dead. So help him. Do not mock me. O do not leave me – O do not move away from me.

O you good, sir - you venerable sir.
O you who draws respect with your kind looks and your advanced years. I am Kisa Gotami and this is my son who is dead. You sir, deserving the respect of one who is an elder – help my son, sir.

Elderly Man

Kisa Gotami, I have heard you now in this market. I cannot help you but I know one who can.

Kisa Gotami

O sir, will my son regain his life?

Elderly Man

Come with me, Kisa Gotami. I am on my way to see the Enlightened One, the Buddha, who is just a short distance from here.
Come with me.
Tell the Buddha yourself your grief.
Ask him for a miracle.
Come, I do not mock you.
Come, I do not tell you to cremate your child. I tell you to see the Buddha, the Enlightened One.

Scene 2
The elderly man's advice

Elderly Man

And then I brought Kisa Gotami to the Enlightened One.

Just a short distance away, a short walk down the streets and then just outside the city walls, below that great tree with its overhanging branches sat the Buddha.

I said to Kisa Gotami: *Go child, go and speak to the Buddha. Go to him with your son and he shall put an end to your grief.*

Will he bring my son back to life? Kisa Gotami asked me.

I said, *Go to the Enlightened One, there where he sits below the tree and he shall put an end to your grief. Go.*

Then I saw her walk before me.

She walked slowly at first. Then she stumbled. Then she ran. She ran straight to that great tree and then she placed her son on the ground before the Buddha.

And she prostrated herself before the Enlightened One. I showed my respect to the Buddha and stood aside while Kisa Gotami spoke to the Enlightened One.

She said: *O Enlightened One, this is my son I have brought to you. The people of Savatthi say he is dead. No one will help us. Give me back my son - alive. Give him life, O Enlightened One.*

Let him live.

And the Buddha looked at Kisa Gotami, and he said, *Gotami, if that is what you desire, go forth to the houses in the city and bring me a handful of mustard seeds given freely to you by a householder whose house has never been visited by death.*

And Kisa Gotami jumped up immediately. She repeated the words of the Buddha quickly: *A handful of mustard seeds, O Enlightened One. Given freely by a householder whose house has never been visited by death.*

And I saw her turn round immediately and she ran. She ran towards the city. And I, I waited for her until she returned from the city.

Scene 3
A handful of mustard seeds

Kisa Gotami

And I ran to the city.

I left my son at the feet of the Buddha and I ran to the city.

I ran as fast as I could, with the words of the Buddha still ringing in my ears.

Go forth to the city, he said.
Go to the houses, he said.
Bring back to me, he said, *a handful of mustard seeds given freely by a householder whose house has never been visited by death.*

O what could be easier?

A handful of mustard seeds for my son's life.
A handful of mustard seeds - O who would not give a handful of mustard seeds?

I ran to the city. I ran as fast as I could.

I knocked at the first door.
I was panting.
I was breathing hard.
The sweat was pouring down my forehead and face.

A woman opened the door.
Old Mother, I said. *Old Mother*, I said to the woman.

Child, said the kind woman. *Who are you, child? What do you want?*

A handful of mustard seeds is all I want. I'm Kisa Gotami. Give me freely a handful of mustard seeds and I shall give them to the Buddha. I shall give them to the Enlightened One and he shall give me my son back alive. A handful of mustard seeds for my son's life, Old Mother.

Wait here, said the woman and within minutes she returned with a bowl of mustard seeds. And she smiled kindly. And she poured the seeds into my cupped hands. I had a handful of mustard seeds. Given freely to me.

May you be happy, child, said the woman.

I nodded, turned round to go, hardly thanking the woman.

Then I remembered.

I turned back to the woman. She was still standing there at the door.
Old Mother, I said. *Old Mother, tell me. The Buddha said I must get this handful of mustard seeds freely form a home that has not seen death.
Has this home seen death, Old Mother?*

The woman was silent for a while and she said, *Only last year my grandchild died, Kisa Gotami. Only last year.*

I poured the seeds back into the bowl.

I must go, I said and I ran. I ran as quickly as I could.

The sweat was pouring down my back and my armpits.

I ran as quickly as I could to the next house.

There were children outside the house. Their mother sat on a low wall watching them, as a hen watches over her chicks.

Help me, I said to the woman.

She looked at me, surprised. And the children stopped their play, and they looked at me.

Help me, I said again.

What is it sister? the woman asked.

And I said, *A handful of mustard seeds is all I want. Give me a handful of mustard seeds and I shall give them to the Buddha. I shall give them to the Enlightened One and he shall give me my son back alive. A handful of mustard seeds for my son's life, dearest sister.*

O what mother will not help you, said the woman. *Quick, Shamini,* she said to one of her children. *Go in and bring my sister here a bowl of mustard seeds.*

And the child did as the mother bade her do.

And the lovely child returned to her mother with a bowl of mustard seeds. And taking the bowl in her hands she poured the seeds into my cupped hands.

Go quickly then, she said to me. *Go and give these seeds to the Noble One. May your child live again and may you be happy.*

Again I had the mustard seeds I needed. A handful of mustard seeds for my son's life.

I turned round and then turned back to the kind sister.

Sister, I said.

Yes, Kisa Gotami, she said.

The Buddha said I must obtain these seeds freely from a home not visited by death before. Has your home been visited by death, sister?

The woman grew sad.

Only two years ago, she said, *only two years ago, I lost one of my five children. The grief has yet to leave me. And only last year the children's grandfather died in his village. Alas, death has visited this home, Kisa Gotami. It has.*

I screamed.

And I dropped the seeds on the ground.

I ran again. I ran further up into the city and I was screaming. I knocked at a door.

I told the householder about my son. I told him about the mustard seeds. And I asked him: *But has death visited your home?*

And I had to leave. And then I went to the next home.

And yet again I left with empty hands.

At the next home they shut the door in my face.
Word had spread.

Word had spread about Kisa Gotami.

Kisa Gotami the mad woman.

Kisa Gotami has lost her son.

She has gone mad.

She goes from home to home asking for mustard seeds. Mustard seeds for her son's life. And then she wants to know if death has visited your home.

Do not open your doors to Kisa Gotami.
Let her scream in the streets.
Let her cry in the streets.

So the word had spread.
No one opened their doors.
I ran from street to street.
Screaming and shouting.

And then I was at a home where there was weeping.

A woman was wailing. Her children were round her, crying.

The doors were open and there were people everywhere, looking somber.

I knew what it was.

Death. Pain. Loss.

The woman was crying for her husband.

He was dead.

Her children were crying for their father.

They clasped the man's corpse and they wept.

I walked back into the streets.

I was not weeping any more.
I was calm.

I walked.

I was not crying any more.

And then the darkness lifted from my heart.
The grief left me.
I kept walking silently.
And I knew what the wise ones knew:

There was no home where death had not visited.
It is the way.
Birth.
Being.
Activity.
Ageing.
Sickness.
Rites of passage.
Stages of life.
Old Age.
Death.
And birth.
And death.
And birth.

And I kept walking.

Endless cycles of birth and death and birth.
Births in all worlds and all dimensions.

I kept walking.
I knew suddenly what the wise ones knew:
Samsara.
The ocean of life and death.
Samsara.
The Ocean of craving, being, birth, life and death.
I knew life. I knew death. I knew now what the wise
knew.
I was now before the Buddha.
I knelt before him and I said: *Lord, O Enlightened One, I*
know now the Noble Truth. And the Noble Truth has
removed sorrow from my heart, Lord.

I picked up my child and I arranged for his cremation.

I did my duty by my child.

For now I knew what the wise ones knew.

Scene 4

Gotami's wisdom

The Elderly Man

And I saw Kisa Gotami come back to the Buddha.

She came back with a glow in her face. She did not come back running and agitated.

She came back slowly with measured steps.

She came with the calm demeanor of one who is wise.

And then she spoke to the Buddha and she said she understood the Noble Truth now.

She received the Buddha's blessing and she left with her son's corpse to do her duty.

And after that, she returned to the Buddha.

She was initiated as a nun.
She joined the order of the nuns.

Kisa Gotami was not known any more as the Thin Gotami.

She became known as a wise woman.

She became known as a noble nun who followed the Dharma.

Epilogue

Epilogue

Buddham Saranam Gacchami
Dhammam Saranam Gacchami
Sangham Saranam Gacchami

O all people who hear this, the story of Kisa Gotami;
O all who hear this story of Kisa Gotami of Savatthi of
the kingdom of Kosala, of ancient India in the time of
the Buddha, the Enlightened One;

O all people who hear of Kisa Gotami, the mother who
suffered the death of her only child and how, in her
suffering, was born her wisdom:

Let us wish all beings happiness and joy.

*May all beings find the means to transcend their
sorrows.*

*May all beings, may all beings in all forms and in all
worlds, may all beings be happy.*

*May all beings acquire the means to wisdom, and may
that wisdom lead them to transcend all pain and sorrow.*

May all beings be happy.

Buddham Saranam Gacchami
Dhammam Saranam Gacchami
Sangham Saranam Gacchami